"It's hard to connect with your child withou[t]
As counselors and speakers at parenting e[vents]
a great deal of time teaching parents abou[t]
child is—not just physically, but emotional[ly]
to truly know and understand *who* your chi[ld]
key to connecting. The Phase Guides give you the tools to do just that. Our wise
friends Reggie and Kristen have put together an insightful, hopeful, practical,
and literal year-by-year guide that will help you to understand and connect with
your child at every age."

SISSY GOFF
*M.ED., LPC-MHSP, DIRECTOR OF CHILD & ADOLESCENT COUNSELING AT DAYSTAR
COUNSELING MINISTRIES IN NASHVILLE, TENNESSEE, SPEAKER AND AUTHOR OF
ARE MY KIDS ON TRACK?*

"These resources for parents are fantastically empowering, absolute in their
simplicity, and completely doable in every way. The hard work that has gone
into the Phase Project will echo through the next generation of children in
powerful ways."

JENNIFER WALKER
RN BSN, AUTHOR AND FOUNDER OF MOMS ON CALL

"We all know where we want to end up in our parenting, but how to get there
can seem like an unsolved mystery. Through the Phase Project series, Reggie
Joiner and Kristen Ivy team up to help us out. The result is a resource that guides
us through the different seasons of raising children, and provides a road map to
parenting in such a way that we finish up with very few regrets."

SANDRA STANLEY
FOSTER CARE ADVOCATE, BLOGGER, WIFE TO ANDY STANLEY, MOTHER OF THREE

"Not only are the Phase Guides the most creative and well-thought-out guides
to parenting I have ever encountered, these books are ESSENTIAL to my
daily parenting. With a 13-year-old, 11-year-old, and 9-year-old at home, I am
swimming in their wake of daily drama and delicacy. These books are a reminder
to enjoy every second. Because it's just a phase."

CARLOS WHITTAKER
AUTHOR, SPEAKER, FATHER OF THREE

"As the founder of Minnie's Food Pantry, I see thousands of people each
month with children who will benefit from the advice, guidance, and nuggets
of information on how to celebrate and understand the phases of their child's
life. Too often we feel like we're losing our mind when sweet little Johnny
starts to change his behavior into a person we do not know. I can't wait to start
implementing the principles of these books with my clients to remind them . . .
it's just a phase."

CHERYL JACKSON
*FOUNDER OF MINNIE'S FOOD PANTRY, AWARD-WINNING PHILANTHROPIST,
AND GRANDMOTHER*

"I began exploring this resource with my counselor hat on, thinking how valuable this will be for the many parents I spend time with in my office. I ended up taking my counselor hat off and putting on my parent hat. Then I kept thinking about friends who are teachers, coaches, youth pastors, and children's ministers, who would want this in their hands. What a valuable resource the Orange team has given us to better understand and care for the kids and adolescents we love. I look forward to sharing it broadly."

DAVID THOMAS
LMSW, DIRECTOR OF FAMILY COUNSELING, DAYSTAR COUNSELING MINISTRIES, SPEAKER AND AUTHOR OF ARE MY KIDS ON TRACK? *AND* WILD THINGS: THE ART OF NURTURING BOYS

"I have always wished someone would hand me a manual for parenting. Well, the Phase Guides are more than what I wished for. They guide, inspire, and challenge me as a parent—while giving me incredible insight into my children at each age and phase. Our family will be using these every year!"

COURTNEY DEFEO
AUTHOR OF IN THIS HOUSE, WE WILL GIGGLE, *MOTHER OF TWO*

"As I speak to high school students and their parents, I always wonder to myself: What would it have been like if they had better seen what was coming next? What if they had a guide that would tell them what to expect and how to be ready? What if they could anticipate what is predictable about the high school years before they actually hit? These Phase Guides give a parent that kind of preparation so they can have a plan when they need it most."

JOSH SHIPP
AUTHOR, TEEN EXPERT, AND YOUTH SPEAKER

"The Phase Guides are incredibly creative, well researched, and filled with inspirational actions for everyday life. Each age-specific guide is catalytic for equipping parents to lead and love their kids as they grow up. I'm blown away and deeply encouraged by the content and by its creators. I highly recommend Phase resources for all parents, teachers, and influencers of children. This is the stuff that challenges us and changes our world. Get them. Read them. And use them!"

DANIELLE STRICKLAND
OFFICER WITH THE SALVATION ARMY, AUTHOR, SPEAKER, MOTHER OF TWO

"It's true that parenting is one of life's greatest joys but it is not without its challenges. If we're honest, parenting can sometimes feel like trying to choreograph a dance to an ever-changing beat. It can be clumsy and riddled with well-meaning missteps. If parenting is a dance, this Parenting Guide is a skilled instructor refining your technique and helping you move gracefully to a steady beat. For those of us who love to plan ahead, this guide will help you anticipate what's to come so you can be poised and ready to embrace the moments you want to enjoy."

TINA NAIDOO
MSSW, LCSW EXECUTIVE DIRECTOR, THE POTTER'S HOUSE OF DALLAS, INC.

PARENTING YOUR THIRD GRADER

A GUIDE TO MAKING THE MOST OF THE "SOUNDS LIKE FUN!" PHASE

KRISTEN IVY AND REGGIE JOINER

PARENTING YOUR THIRD GRADER
A GUIDE TO MAKING THE MOST OF THE
"SOUNDS LIKE FUN!" PHASE

Published by Orange, a division of The reThink Group, Inc.,
5870 Charlotte Lane, Suite 300,
Cumming, GA 30040 U.S.A.

©2017 The Phase Project
Authors: Kristen Ivy and Reggie Joiner
Lead Editor: Karen Wilson
Editing Team: Melanie Williams, Hannah Crosby, Sherry Surratt

Art Direction: Ryan Boon and Hannah Crosby
Book Design: FiveStone and Sharon van Rossum
Project Manager : Nate Brandt

Printed in the United States of America
First Edition 2017
10 11 12 13 14 15 16 17 18 19

12/4/2019

Special thanks to:

Jim Burns, Ph.D for guidance and consultation on having conversations about sexual integrity

Jon Acuff for guidance and consultation on having conversations about technological responsibility

Jean Sumner, MD for guidance and consultation on having conversations about healthy habits

Every educator, counselor, community leader, and researcher who invested in the Phase Project

TABLE OF CONTENTS

HOW TO USE THIS ~~BOOK~~ ~~JOURNAL~~ GUIDE

The guide you hold in your hand doesn't have very many words, but it does have a lot of ideas. Some of these ideas come from thousands of hours of research. Others come from parents, educators, and volunteers who spend every day with kids the same age as yours. This guide won't tell you everything about your kid, but it will tell you a few things about kids at this age.

The best way to use this guide is to take what these pages tell you about third graders and combine it with what you know is true about *your* third grader.

Let's sum it up:

THINGS ABOUT THIRD GRADERS +
THOUGHTS ABOUT *YOUR* THIRD GRADER =
YOUR GUIDE TO THE NEXT 52 WEEKS OF PARENTING

After each idea in this guide, there are pages with a few questions designed to prompt you to think about your kid, your family, and yourself as a parent. The only guarantee we give to parents who use this guide is this: You will mess up some things as a parent this year. Actually, that's a guarantee to every parent, regardless. But you, you picked up this book! You want to be a better parent. And that's what we hope this guide will do: help you parent your kid just a little better, simply because you paused to consider a few ideas that can help you make the most of this phase.

THE THIRD GRADE PHASE

Third grade is a year of beautiful discovery and soul-shaping challenges. It's a season of adventure for both you and your child.

Most third graders still have a child's innocent enthusiasm for life that allows them to embrace new experiences. It's not without reason the catch phrase for this phase is "Sounds like fun!" Most third graders just have a naturally optimistic outlook.

And your child will need this optimism as they enter this school year with some very real educational challenges. For many kids, third grade is the year of fractions, multiplication tables, and grammar rules. This may also be the year your child's mind awakens to the joy of reading for pleasure. Whether they're into comic books, fan-fiction, or classic favorites, hours can fly by as they devour book after book until the mystery is solved or the hero triumphs over evil.

Whatever this phase brings academically, your posture of encouragement, support, and unwavering love will set a positive tone for a future of life-long learning.

Most third graders are also blossoming in their social connections. The relationships they have with friends and other leaders outside of your family may begin to take on greater meaning this year. They may even have a best friend.

Of all the characteristics associated with third grade, it's this social aspect I remember as the most formative part of my own third-grade experience. At that time, my family was living in Nicaragua, where my dad was engineering a major infrastructure development project. I was blessed to grow up in a family that loved Jesus. Giving my life to Him at a young age was the most natural thing for me to do. But it was in the third grade when I began to make friends who had a different value system. My social interactions during this phase introduced thoughts and actions that were, for the first time, incongruent with my faith. And, as I recall, my third-grade year saw more parent/teacher meetings than any other!

I can't tell you how thankful I am for the tribe of Jesus-followers who God placed in my life during that time. From my parents, to caring adults at church, to my third-grade teacher at school—each played a pivotal role as I navigated a critical time in my life. I was fortunate to belong to a strong community of believers who greatly influenced my life as I learned to wade in the new waters of social pressure.

Perhaps it was that personal experience that led me to so passionately embrace a holistic approach to discipleship with my own children. This approach combined Biblically-based content with life-giving relationships, the development of spiritual practices, and intentional planning around extraordinary experiences.

As you and your child enter this important third-grade phase, I pray that the new information and content you engage this year will be transformational. I pray you will be supported by strong relationships that surround you with wise counsel and good company. I pray you will enjoy extraordinary experiences together that God will use to help your child become more like Jesus. And I pray that the rhythms of your family's routines will incorporate spiritual practices that encourage your child to love and follow Jesus through these amazing, adventurous 52 weeks that stretch before you, and on into eternity.

- SANTIAGO "JIMMY" MELLADO
PRESIDENT AND CEO OF COMPASSION INTERNATIONAL

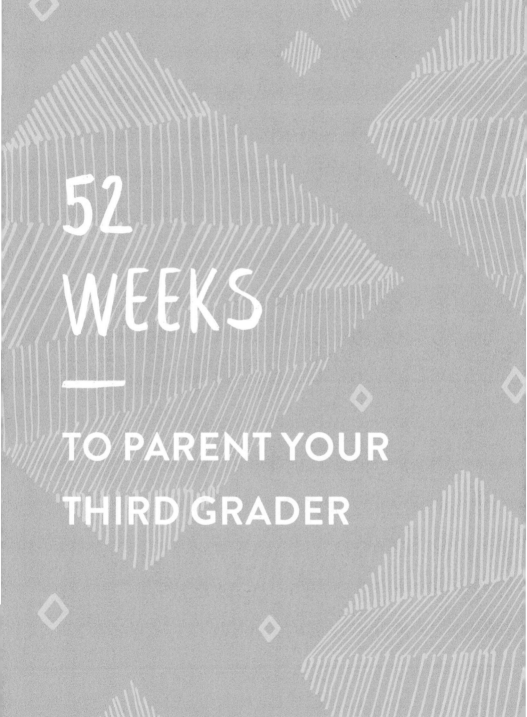

52 WEEKS

TO PARENT YOUR THIRD GRADER

WHEN YOU SEE
HOW MUCH

Time

YOU HAVE LEFT

—

YOU TEND TO DO

More

WITH THE TIME
YOU HAVE NOW.

THERE ARE APPROXIMATELY

936 WEEKS

FROM THE TIME A BABY IS BORN
UNTIL THEY GROW UP AND MOVE TO
WHATEVER IS NEXT.

On the day your child starts third grade, you have 520 weeks remaining. Your kid is now halfway through elementary school, and things like cell phone contracts and learner's permits are much closer than they seem. Your kid is growing up faster than you ever dreamed.

That's why every week counts. Of course, each week might not feel significant. There may be weeks this year when all you feel like you accomplished was reminding them to finish their science project—the night before it was due. That's okay.

Take a deep breath.
You don't have to get everything done this week.

But what happens in your child's life week after week, year after year, adds up over time. So, it might be a good idea to put a number to your weeks.

MEASURE IT OUT.

Write down the number of weeks that have already passed since your child was born. Then write down the number of weeks you have left before they graduate high school.

HINT: If you want a little help counting it out, you can download the free Parent Cue app on all mobile platforms.

_____

_____

_____

CREATE A VISUAL COUNTDOWN.

Find a jar and fill it with one marble for each week you have remaining with your child. Then make a habit of removing one marble every week as a reminder to make the most of your time. Where can you place your visual countdown so you will see it frequently?

_____

_____

_____

_____

Which day of the week is best for you to remove a marble?

_____

_____

_____

Is there anything you want to do each week as you remove a marble? (Examples: say a prayer, play a game, retell one favorite memory from this past week)

_____

_____

_____

_____

_____

_____

_____

_____

_____

_____

_____

_____

_____

EVERY PHASE IS A
TIMEFRAME
IN A KID'S LIFE
WHEN YOU CAN
LEVERAGE
DISTINCTIVE
OPPORTUNITIES
TO INFLUENCE
THEIR

future.

YOU ONLY HAVE
52 WEEKS
WITH YOUR THIRD GRADER

while they are still in third grade.

Then they will be in fourth grade,

and you will never know them as a third grader again.

Or, to say it another way:

Before you know it, your kid will grow up a little more and . . .

really care what brand you buy.

see something online you hadn't counted on.

ask for a cell phone (if they haven't already).

The point is this: The phase you are in now has remarkable potential. And before the end of third grade, there are some distinctive opportunities you don't want to miss. So as you count down the next 52 weeks, pay attention to what makes these weeks uniquely different from the time you've already spent together and the weeks you will have when they move on to the next phase.

What are some things you have noticed about your third grader in this phase that you really enjoy?

_____

_____

_____

_____

_____

_____

_____

_____

_____

_____

_____

_____

_____

_____

_____

_____

_____

_____

_____

What is something new you are learning as a parent during this phase?

_____

_____

_____

_____

_____

_____

_____

_____

_____

_____

_____

_____

_____

_____

_____

_____

_____

_____

_____

_____

_____

THIRD GRADE

—

THE PHASE WHEN FAIRNESS MATTERS MOST, DIFFERENCES GET NOTICED, AND YOUR ENTHUSIASTIC KID THINKS ANYTHING, *"Sounds like fun!"*

FAIRNESS MATTERS.

The world of your third grader is highly defined. Things are right or they are wrong. Someone is either good, or they are bad. And if you happen to give someone else the larger slice, you will find out pretty quickly to which category you belong.

DIFFERENCES DISPLAY THEIR UNIQUENESS.

Your third grader's brain is changing in some incredible ways. They are developing their ability to empathize, but they are still quick to put people (including themselves) into categories. They may be quick to let you know, for example, if they are "athletic" or "not athletic."

THIS PHASE IS A BLEND OF CAPABLE AND DEPENDENT.

You are still in the golden age of childhood. No one should have a favorite phase, but if you like this phase a whole lot, you aren't alone. Your kid is impressionable, enthusiastic, and excited about what you are excited about. If you think something sounds like fun, it won't take much to convince them it really is fun. (That may not be as easy in a few years.)

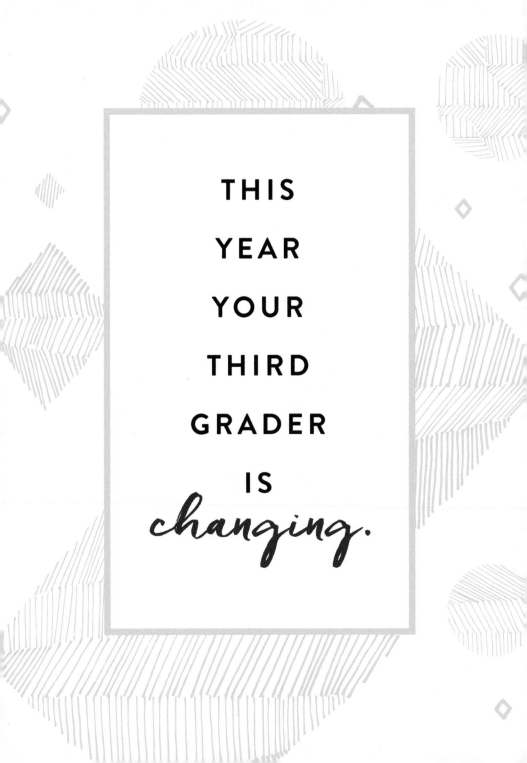

THIS
YEAR
YOUR
THIRD
GRADER
IS
changing.

PHYSICALLY

- Continues losing baby teeth including molars (9-12 years)
- Grows approximately three inches and gains seven pounds, in spurts
- Improving hand-eye coordination
- Plays hard, tires quickly, and benefits from short "breaks"
- Needs 10-11 hours of sleep

SOCIALLY

- Enjoys cooperative, group activities
- Places a high value on fairness and consistency
- Shows gender preference for friends
- Starts to gather in larger friend groups and responds to peer pressure

MENTALLY

- Concentrates on one activity up to 30 minutes
- Increasingly aware of the feelings of others
- Recognizes patterns & symbolism
- May enjoy reading books both for fun and for learning
- Focuses on one thing at a time and struggles with abstract concepts
- Has a highly definitive perspective (things are either right or wrong)

EMOTIONALLY

- Tends to be enthusiastic, energetic, and impatient
- Overall feels more independent and confident
- Developing their sense of humor with riddles, magic tricks, and jokes
- May be quick to label themselves ("athletic" vs. "not athletic". . .)
- Needs to experience moderate challenges and success

What are some changes you are noticing in your third grader?

_____

_____

_____

_____

_____

_____

_____

You may disagree with some of the characteristics we've shared about third graders. That's because every third grader is unique. What makes your third grader different from third graders in general?

_____

_____

_____

_____

_____

_____

_____

_____

What do you want to remember about this year with your third grader?

Mark this page. Throughout the year, write down a few simple things you want to remember. If you want to be really thorough, there are about 52 blank lines. But some weeks, you may spend so much time trying to figure out who else is going to the slumber party that you forget to write down a memory. That's okay.

_____

_____

_____

_____

_____

_____

_____

_____

_____

_____

_____

_____

_____

_____

_____

_____

_____

_____

_____

SIX THINGS
—
EVERY KID
NEEDS

YOUR KID NEEDS **6** THINGS OVER TIME

LOVE

WORDS

WORK

TRIBES

STORIES

FUN

OVER THE NEXT 520 WEEKS, YOUR CHILD WILL NEED MANY THINGS:

Some of the things your kid needs will change from phase to phase, but there are six things every kid needs at every phase. In fact, these things may be the most important things you give your kid.

EVERY KID, AT EVERY PHASE, NEEDS . . .

♡ LOVE
to give them a
sense of WORTH.

📖 STORIES
to give them a bigger
PERSPECTIVE.

WORK
to give them
SIGNIFICANCE.

♟ FUN
to give them
CONNECTION.

👪 TRIBES
to give them
BELONGING.

💬 WORDS
to give them
DIRECTION.

The next few pages are designed to help you think about how you will give your child these six things, right now—while they are in third grade.

EVERY KID

NEEDS

love

OVER TIME

—

TO GIVE THEM

A SENSE OF

worth.

ONE QUESTION YOUR
THIRD GRADER IS ASKING

Your third grader is keen for comparison. They love to compare movies, sports teams, ice cream flavors . . . and people. This tendency often leaves kids wondering just how well they measure up.

Your third grader is asking one major question:

"DO I HAVE WHAT IT TAKES?"

So pay attention to their efforts and interests. Whether your third grader develops greater proficiency at sports, music, or solving a Rubik's Cube® in under 60 seconds, they still need you to do one thing:

ENGAGE their interests.

Your third grader notices the way you notice them. So, engage your third grader's interests by . . .

showing curiosity about their activities,

encouraging their efforts,

and helping them push through setbacks.

You are probably doing more than you realize to show your third grader just how much you love them. Make a list of the ways you already show up consistently to engage your child's interests.

You may need to look at this list on a bad day to remember what a great parent you are.

_____

_____

_____

_____

_____

_____

_____

_____

_____

_____

_____

_____

_____

_____

_____

_____

Engaging your child's interests requires paying attention to what they like. What does your third grader seem to enjoy the most right now?

_____

_____

_____

_____

_____

_____

_____

_____

_____

_____

_____

_____

_____

_____

_____

_____

_____

_____

_____

It's impossible to love anyone with the persistence a third grader requires unless you have a little time for yourself. What can you do to refuel each week so you are able to give your third grader the love they need?

_____

_____

_____

_____

_____

_____

_____

_____

_____

_____

_____

_____

_____

_____

_____

_____

_____

_____

Who do you have around you supporting you this year?

_____

_____

_____

_____

_____

_____

_____

_____

_____

_____

_____

_____

_____

_____

_____

_____

_____

_____

_____

_____

_____

EVERY KID

NEEDS

stories

OVER TIME

—

TO GIVE THEM

A BIGGER

perspective.

BOOKS TO READ
WITH YOUR THIRD GRADER

MR. POPPER'S PENGUINS
by Richard Atwater

THE ONE AND ONLY IVAN
by Katherine Applegate

THE TALES OF DIMWOOD FOREST (SERIES)
by Avi

THE PENDERWICKS (SERIES)
by Jeanne Birdsall

FRINDLE
by Andrew Clements

CHARLIE AND THE CHOCOLATE FACTORY
by Roald Dahl

HEREVILLE: HOW MIRKA GOT HER SWORD
by Barry Deusch

THE MIRACULOUS JOURNEY OF EDWARD TULANE
by Kate DiCamillo

ZITA THE SPACE GIRL
by Ben Hatke

NANCY DREW (SERIES)
by Carolyn Keene

THE JUNGLE BOOK
by Rudyard Kipling

PIPPI LONGSTOCKING
by Astrid Lindgren

WHEN WE WERE VERY YOUNG
by A. A. Milne

ISLAND OF THE BLUE DOLPHINS
by Scott O'Dell

THE BEST CHRISTMAS PAGEANT EVER
by Barbara Robinson

HARRY POTTER (BOOKS 1-3)
by J.K. Rowling

SIDEWAYS STORIES FROM WAYSIDE SCHOOL
by Louis Sachar and Julie Brinckloe

SMILE
by Raina Telgemeier

STUART LITTLE
by E.B. White

WHO WAS (SERIES)
by multiple authors

Tell your third grader's story. What are some moments you want to re-tell?

Think of times you saw your third grader doing something good, times you both learned something new, or maybe a special time when you had fun together.

_____

_____

_____

_____

_____

_____

_____

_____

_____

_____

_____

_____

_____

_____

_____

_____

_____

_____

How might you share grandparent or great-grandparent stories with your third grader? If you have an adopted or foster child, how might you talk about and celebrate your child's ancestral family?

_____

_____

_____

_____

_____

_____

_____

_____

_____

_____

_____

_____

_____

_____

_____

_____

_____

_____

Tell your family story. What do you want to record now so you can share it with your third grader later? Consider starting a family journal, a video archive, a travel scrapbook, or a drawer of things connected to special memories. Write down some ideas that might fit your family's values and style.

_____

_____

_____

_____

_____

_____

_____

_____

_____

_____

_____

_____

_____

_____

_____

_____

EVERY KID

NEEDS

work

OVER TIME

—

TO GIVE

THEM

significance.

WORK YOUR
THIRD GRADER CAN DO

BANDAGE A CUT

**GATHER TRASH BAGS
FROM AROUND
THE HOUSE**

RAKE LEAVES
(if that's a thing where you live)

UNPACK A LUNCH BOX

EMPTY THE DISHWASHER

PUT AWAY DISHES

BOIL PASTA

**SORT, WASH, FOLD AND
PUT AWAY LAUNDRY**

HELP WASH THE CAR

**PLANT AND WATER
FLOWERS**

**MAKE A GRILLED
CHEESE SANDWICH**

**MAKE THE BED AND
CLEAN THEIR ROOM**
(even if it doesn't always
stay that way)

What are some jobs you can give to your third grader?

Some days it's easier than others to motivate your third grader to do their work. What are some strategies that tend to keep your third grader motivated?

HINT: Maybe try a few things like, "You can choose what / where we eat on Friday."

_____

_____

_____

_____

_____

_____

_____

_____

_____

_____

_____

_____

_____

_____

_____

_____

_____

What are things you hope your third grader will be able to do independently in the next phase?

_____

_____

_____

_____

_____

_____

_____

_____

_____

_____

_____

_____

_____

_____

_____

_____

_____

_____

_____

How are you helping them develop those skills now?

_____

_____

_____

_____

_____

_____

_____

_____

_____

_____

_____

_____

_____

_____

_____

_____

_____

_____

_____

_____

_____

_____

EVERY KID

NEEDS

fun

OVER TIME

—

TO GIVE

THEM

connection.

WAYS TO HAVE FUN WITH YOUR THIRD GRADER

GAMES:

CLUE®

HEDBANZ®

MONOPOLY®

GUESS WHO? ®

BATTLESHIP®

BOGGLE®

QUIRKLE®

PICTIONARY®

SEQUENCE®

CHECKERS

CHESS

THE GAME OF LIFE®

CATAN®

FARKLE®

RACK-O®

TICKET TO RIDE®

MASTERMIND®

BANANAGRAMS®

ACTIVITIES:

RAGE, HIT THE DECK
(card games)

SPOONS
(card game)

CRAFTS WITH BEADS
OR STRING

ART OF ANY KIND
(colored pencils,
markers, paint,
stencils)

FOUR SQUARE

CHARADES

HANGMAN

DOTS

FREEZE TAG

MAD LIBS®

KARAOKE

PAPER FOOTBALL

PAPER AIRPLANES

WATER BALLOONS

WATER GAMES
(Marco Polo)

LEGOS®

100-PIECE
JIGSAW PUZZLES

HONEY, I LOVE
YOU, BUT I JUST
CAN'T SMILE

"FOXES AND
HOUNDS"
(when friends
come over)

What are some games and activities you and your third grader enjoy?

_____

_____

_____

_____

_____

_____

_____

_____

_____

_____

_____

_____

_____

_____

_____

_____

_____

_____

_____

_____

When are the best times of the day, or week, for you to set aside to just have fun with your third grader?

_____

_____

_____

_____

_____

_____

_____

_____

_____

_____

_____

_____

_____

_____

_____

_____

_____

_____

_____

Some days are *extra* fun days. What are some ways you want to celebrate the special days coming up this year?

CHILD'S BIRTHDAY

_____

_____

_____

_____

_____

_____

_____

_____

_____

_____

_____

_____

_____

_____

_____

_____

_____

HOLIDAYS

EVERY KID

NEEDS

tribes

OVER TIME

—

TO GIVE

THEM

belonging.

ADULTS WHO MIGHT INFLUENCE YOUR THIRD GRADER

PARENTS

NEIGHBORS

CHURCH LEADERS

GRANDPARENTS

PARENT'S FRIENDS

COACHES

AUNTS & UNCLES

THIRD GRADE TEACHER

SCHOOL WORKERS

List at least five adults who have influence in your third grader's life right now.

HINT: If you aren't sure, you can ask them.

_____

_____

_____

_____

_____

_____

_____

_____

_____

_____

_____

_____

_____

_____

_____

_____

_____

_____

_____

What is one way these adults could help you and your third grader this year?

_____

_____

_____

_____

_____

_____

_____

_____

_____

_____

_____

_____

_____

_____

_____

_____

_____

_____

_____

What are a few ways you could show these adults appreciation for the significant role they play in your child's life?

_____

_____

_____

_____

_____

_____

_____

_____

_____

_____

_____

_____

_____

_____

_____

_____

_____

_____

_____

EVERY KID

NEEDS

words

OVER TIME

—

TO GIVE

THEM

direction.

WORDS YOUR THIRD GRADER NEEDS TO HEAR

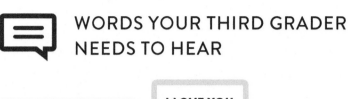

GOOD MORNING!

I LOVE YOU

I HAVE NOTICED . . .

I HOPE YOU KNOW . . .

HAVE FUN

KEEP TRYING

I'M REALLY PROUD WHEN . . .

PLEASE

THANK YOU

WORK HARD

I'VE BEEN THINKING . . .

GOOD NIGHT!

I'M SORRY

BE KIND

I ENJOY SPENDING TIME WITH YOU

I CAN ALWAYS COUNT ON YOU TO . . .

If words over time give a kid direction, what word (or words) describes your hopes for your third grader in this phase?

DETERMINED	MOTIVATED	GENTLE
ENCOURAGING	INTROSPECTIVE	PASSIONATE
SELF-ASSURED	ENTHUSIASTIC	PATIENT
ASSERTIVE	JOYFUL	FORGIVING
DARING	ENTERTAINING	CREATIVE
INSIGHTFUL	INDEPENDENT	WITTY
COMPASSIONATE	OBSERVANT	AMBITIOUS
AMIABLE	SENSITIVE	HELPFUL
EASY-GOING	ENDEARING	AUTHENTIC
DILIGENT	ADVENTUROUS	INVENTIVE
PROACTIVE	HONEST	DEVOTED
OPTIMISTIC	CURIOUS	GENUINE
FEARLESS	DEPENDABLE	ATTENTIVE
AFFECTIONATE	GENEROUS	HARMONIOUS
COURAGEOUS	COMMITTED	EMPATHETIC
CAUTIOUS	RESPONSIBLE	COURAGEOUS
DEVOTED	TRUSTWORTHY	FLEXIBLE
INQUISITIVE	THOUGHTFUL	CAREFUL
PATIENT	LOYAL	NURTURING
OPEN-MINDED	KIND	RELIABLE

Where can you place those words in your home so they will remind you what you want for your child this year?

_____

_____

_____

_____

_____

_____

_____

_____

_____

_____

_____

_____

_____

_____

_____

_____

_____

_____

_____

_____

The words we use determine the way we think. Are there words you have chosen not to say *(or not to say often)*? What do you want your kid to know about these words, and how do you want them to respond if they hear them?

_____

_____

_____

_____

_____

_____

_____

_____

_____

_____

_____

_____

_____

_____

_____

_____

_____

_____

FOUR
CONVERSATIONS
—

TO HAVE IN THIS PHASE

WHEN YOU KNOW
WHERE YOU WANT
TO GO,

AND YOU KNOW
WHERE YOU ARE
NOW,

YOU CAN ALWAYS
DO SOMETHING

TO MOVE IN A
BETTER DIRECTION.

→

OVER THE NEXT 520 WEEKS OF YOUR CHILD'S LIFE, SOME CONVERSATIONS MAY MATTER MORE THAN OTHERS.

WHAT YOU SAY, FOR EXAMPLE, REGARDING . . .	MIGHT HAVE LESS IMPACT ON THEIR FUTURE THAN WHAT YOU SAY REGARDING . . .
Star Wars	Health
Shark attacks	Sex
and Justin Timberlake	Technology
	or Faith.

The next pages are about the conversations that matter most. On the left page is a destination—what you might want to be true in your kid's life 520 weeks from now. On the right page is a goal for conversations with your third grader and a few suggestions about what you might want to say.

Healthy habits

—

LEARNING TO
STRENGTHEN
MY BODY THROUGH
EXERCISE, NUTRITION,
AND SELF-ADVOCACY

THIS YEAR YOU WILL

DEVELOP POSITIVE ROUTINES

SO YOUR CHILD WILL ENJOY EATING WELL AND EXERCISING OFTEN.

Maintain a good relationship with your pediatrician, and schedule a well visit at least once per year. You can also begin to develop healthy habits for your third grader with a few simple words.

SAY THINGS LIKE . . .

I LOVE TO WATCH YOU PLAY!

THE MAYONNAISE CAN'T SIT IN THE SUN ALL DAY.
(Teach food safety.)

CAN YOU SEE HOW MUCH SODIUM IS IN THIS CAN?
(Teach your kid to read labels and evaluate the nutrition value of food.)

LET'S PLAY FREEZE FRISBEE.

SOME PEOPLE ARE NATURALLY BETTER JUMPERS, BUT WE CAN ALL JUMP HIGHER WITH PRACTICE.
(Encourage them to keep trying to improve.)

What are some activities you can do with your third grader that require a little bit of exercise? *(They may not call it exercise, but if you get a little winded that counts.)*

_____

_____

_____

_____

_____

_____

_____

_____

_____

_____

_____

_____

_____

_____

_____

_____

_____

_____

Kids who cook learn about what ingredients are in the things they eat. What are some simple ways your third grader can help you in the kitchen?

_____

_____

_____

_____

_____

_____

_____

_____

_____

_____

_____

_____

_____

_____

_____

_____

_____

_____

Who will help you monitor and improve your third grader's health?

_____

_____

_____

_____

_____

_____

_____

_____

_____

_____

_____

_____

_____

_____

_____

_____

_____

_____

_____

_____

_____

_____

What are your own health goals for this year? How can you improve the habits in your own life—*you know, even if more meals than you'd like to admit come from a drive-thru window?*

_____

_____

_____

_____

_____

_____

_____

_____

_____

_____

_____

_____

_____

_____

_____

_____

_____

_____

Sexual integrity

—

GUARDING MY
POTENTIAL FOR
INTIMACY THROUGH
APPROPRIATE
BOUNDARIES
AND MUTUAL
RESPECT

THIS YEAR YOU WILL

INFORM THEM ABOUT HOW THINGS WORK

SO YOUR CHILD WILL UNDERSTAND BIOLOGY
AND BUILD SOCIAL SKILLS.

Your third grader may begin expressing a desire for more privacy as they change or bathe. (Kids grow at their own pace. Some kids begin body changes much earlier than others.) Respond to your child's signals by respecting their privacy, but don't disengage. Your third grader needs your influence as they grow to discover more and ask more about sexuality.

SAY THINGS LIKE . . .

> **YOU ARE BEAUTIFUL / HANDSOME JUST THE WAY YOU ARE.**

"CAN WE TALK MORE ABOUT THIS ANOTHER TIME?"
(Always finish the conversation with room to pick it back up again later.)

> **WHAT DO YOUR FRIENDS SAY ABOUT SEX?**

"SEX IS PRIVATE, IT'S NOT SOMETHING WE WATCH OR LOOK AT."

"HAVE YOU HEARD WORDS THAT DESCRIBE BODY PARTS OR SEX THAT YOU DIDN'T UNDERSTAND OR THAT DIDN'T SEEM NICE?"
(Talk about how our language shapes how we think about sex.)

"WHEN A GIRL STARTS TO BECOME A WOMAN, SHE WILL . . . "

"WHEN A BOY STARTS TO BECOME A MAN, HE WILL . . . "

"IT'S NATURAL TO BE CURIOUS ABOUT OUR BODIES."

When it comes to your child's sexuality, what do you hope is true for them 520 weeks from now?

_____

_____

_____

_____

_____

_____

_____

_____

_____

_____

_____

_____

_____

_____

_____

_____

_____

_____

_____

_____

Write down a few things you want to communicate to your third grader about body changes, about sex, and about marriage. *(You don't have to tell them everything now, or in one talk. This should be many talks—over time.)*

For a little help, check out resources like *How God Makes Babies* by Dr. Jim Burns, *Simple Truths* by Mary Flo Ridley, or (for girls) *The Care and Keeping of You* by Valorie Schaefer.

_____

_____

_____

_____

_____

_____

_____

_____

_____

_____

_____

_____

_____

_____

_____

_____

_____

Follow up. Anytime you talk to your third grader about sex, you may walk away feeling like there were things you didn't say that you wish you would have said, or things you said that you wish you had said better. Use this space to reflect. What do you want to communicate better next time?

_____

_____

_____

_____

_____

_____

_____

_____

_____

_____

_____

_____

_____

_____

_____

_____
_____
_____
_____
_____
_____
_____
_____
_____
_____
_____
_____
_____
_____
_____
_____
_____
_____
_____
_____
_____
_____
_____
_____

Technological responsibility

—

LEVERAGING THE POTENTIAL OF ONLINE EXPERIENCES TO ENHANCE MY OFFLINE COMMUNITY AND SUCCESS

THIS YEAR YOU WILL

EXPLORE THE POSSIBILITIES

SO YOUR CHILD WILL UNDERSTAND CORE VALUES AND BUILD ONLINE SKILLS.

Your third grader is smarter than you when it comes to devices—it's okay. That's normal. But even though your kid is a digital native, they still need an adult guide as they continue to explore all the great things they can do with technology.

SAY THINGS LIKE . . .

"LET ME SEE WHAT YOU DID."
(If you have a home computer, put it in a public place, and use positive words to check in and show that you are interested in what they're doing.)

"NEVER POST A PHONE NUMBER OR ADDRESS WITHOUT CHECKING WITH ME."
(Kids are often naïve about sharing personal content with strangers.)

"YOU HAVE ___ MINUTES OF SCREEN TIME FOR TODAY."
(Set limits for screen time and stick to them.)

CAN WE PLAY TOGETHER?
(Make technology social by playing online games together.)

HAVE YOU SEEN ANYTHING ONLINE THAT SURPRISED YOU?

"WHAT IS THE CONTENT RATING? WHAT IS THE COMMITMENT LEVEL? WHAT IS THE CONNECTION TO OTHER PLAYERS?"
(Ask three questions about online games.)

When it comes to your child's engagement with technology, what do you hope is true for them 520 weeks from now?

_____

_____

_____

_____

_____

_____

_____

_____

_____

_____

_____

_____

_____

_____

_____

_____

_____

_____

_____

What rules do you have for digital devices in your family? If you don't have any, what are two or three you might want to set for your third grader?

_____

_____

_____

_____

_____

_____

_____

_____

_____

_____

_____

_____

_____

_____

_____

_____

_____

_____

_____

_____

What are your own personal values and disciplines when it comes to leveraging technology? Are there ways you want to improve your own savvy, skill, or responsibility in this area?

_____

_____

_____

_____

_____

_____

_____

_____

_____

_____

_____

_____

_____

_____

_____

_____

_____

_____

LET'S TALK ABOUT THE PHONE.

They are probably already asking, but you are probably not ready. So, sometime when your third grader isn't around to pressure you, here are a few things to consider:

What are the honest pros and cons of giving your kid a phone some day?

_____

_____

_____

_____

_____

_____

_____

_____

_____

_____

_____

_____

_____

_____

_____

When do you feel is the ideal age to give your kid a phone? *(You will need to know the answer as you negotiate with your third grader, because you can bet they know what they think the ideal age is.)*

_____

_____

_____

_____

_____

What are some ways you want to restrict the access on their phone initially?

If you aren't sure, check out our free cell phone guide at ParentCue.org/CellPhoneGuide. Or do a quick Google search for more ideas. Then write your own thoughts below.

_____

_____

_____

_____

_____

_____

How can you set expectations so your kid knows they can earn
more freedom over time?

_____

_____

_____

_____

_____

_____

_____

_____

_____

_____

_____

_____

_____

_____

_____

_____

_____

_____

_____

Authentic faith

—

TRUSTING JESUS

IN A WAY THAT

TRANSFORMS HOW

I LOVE GOD,

MYSELF,

AND THE REST

OF THE WORLD

THIS YEAR YOU WILL
PROVOKE DISCOVERY
SO YOUR CHILD WILL TRUST GOD'S CHARACTER
AND EXPERIENCE GOD'S FAMILY.

As your third grader gains more independence, this is a great year to encourage personal devotional time. Help them develop a habit of spending time alone with God. But, don't let their faith become private; continue having other faith conversations as you go about your days together.

SAY THINGS LIKE . . .

"CAN I PRAY ABOUT THAT WITH YOU?"

"HAVING FAITH ISN'T ALWAYS EASY, BUT WE CAN TRUST GOD NO MATTER WHAT."

"WHAT DO YOU THINK IS THE WISEST CHOICE IN THIS SITUATION?"

"IF YOU WERE THEM, HOW DO YOU THINK YOU WOULD WANT TO BE TREATED?"

"I'M SORRY YOUR FRIEND'S MOM IS SICK. WHAT COULD WE DO TO HELP?"
(Make service personal. Encourage them to serve people who matter to them.)

"DON'T EVER GET TIRED OF DOING THE RIGHT THING."
2 Thessalonians 3:13
(Repeat and memorize simple Bible verses together.)

"EXODUS IS PART OF THE HISTORY OF THE ISRAELITE NATION."

"DID YOU KNOW THE BOOK OF JAMES WAS WRITTEN BY THE BROTHER OF JESUS?"
(Talk about the Bible.)

"I'M NOT SURE WHERE THAT PASSAGE IS. LET'S LOOK IT UP TOGETHER. "
(Teach them to use a concordance and digital reference tools.)

When it comes to your kid's faith, what do you hope is true for them 520 weeks from now?

_____

_____

_____

_____

_____

_____

_____

_____

_____

_____

_____

_____

_____

_____

_____

_____

_____

_____

_____

What adults are helping influence and develop your third grader's faith?

_____

_____

_____

_____

_____

_____

_____

_____

_____

_____

_____

_____

_____

_____

_____

_____

_____

_____

_____

_____

What routines or habits do you have in your own life that are stretching your faith?

_____

_____

_____

_____

_____

_____

_____

_____

_____

_____

_____

_____

_____

_____

_____

_____

_____

_____

_____

_____

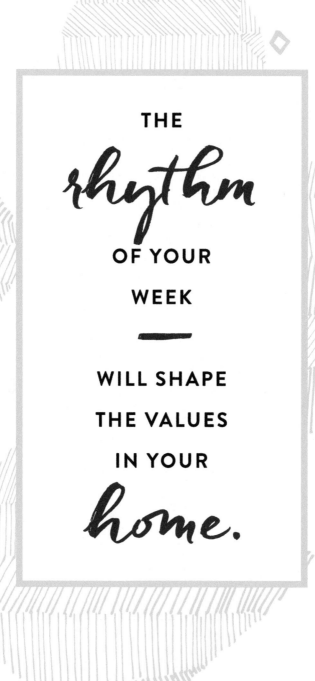

THE

rhythm

OF YOUR

WEEK

—

WILL SHAPE

THE VALUES

IN YOUR

home.

NOW THAT YOU HAVE FILLED THIS BOOK WITH IDEAS AND GOALS, IT MAY SEEM AS IF YOU WILL NEVER HAVE TIME TO GET IT ALL DONE.

Actually, you have *520 weeks.*

And every week has potential.

The secret to making the most of this phase with your third grader is to take advantage of the time you already have. Create a rhythm to your weeks by leveraging these four times together.

Be a coach.
Instill purpose by starting the day with encouraging words.

Be a friend.
Interpret life during informal conversations as you travel.

Be a teacher.
Establish values with intentional conversations while you eat together.

Be a counselor.
Strengthen your relationship through heart conversations at the end of the day.

What are some of your favorite routines with your third grader?

_____

_____

_____

_____

_____

_____

_____

_____

_____

_____

_____

_____

_____

_____

_____

_____

_____

_____

_____

_____

_____

_____

_____

_____

Write down any other thoughts or questions you have about parenting your third grader.

_____

_____

_____

_____

_____

_____

_____

_____

_____

_____

_____

_____

_____

_____

_____

_____

_____

_____

_____

_____

YOU HAVE

APPROXIMATELY

520 WEEKS.

IT'S JUST

A PHASE

SO DON'T

MISS IT.

ABOUT THE AUTHORS

KRISTEN IVY @kristen_ivy

Kristen Ivy is executive director of the Phase Project. She and her husband, Matt, are in the preschool and elementary phases with three kids: Sawyer, Hensley, and Raleigh.

Kristen earned her Bachelors of Education from Baylor University in 2004 and received a Master of Divinity from Mercer University in 2009. She worked in the public school system as a high school biology and English teacher, where she learned firsthand the importance of influencing the next generation.

Kristen is also the executive director of messaging at Orange and has played an integral role in the development of the elementary, middle school, and high school curriculum and has shared her experiences at speaking events across the country. She is the co-author of *Playing for Keeps, Creating a Lead Small Culture, It's Just a Phase,* and *Don't Miss It.*

REGGIE JOINER @reggiejoiner

Reggie Joiner is founder and CEO of the reThink Group and co-founder of the Phase Project. He and his wife, Debbie, have reared four kids into adulthood. They now also have two grandchildren.

The reThink Group (also known as Orange) is a non-profit organization whose purpose is to influence those who influence the next generation. Orange provides resources and training for churches and organizations that create environments for parents, kids, and teenagers.

Before starting the reThink Group in 2006, Reggie was one of the founders of North Point Community Church. During his 11 years with Andy Stanley, Reggie was the executive director of family ministry, where he developed a new concept for relevant ministry to children, teenagers, and married adults. Reggie has authored and co-authored more than 10 books including: *Think Orange, Seven Practices of Effective Ministry, Parenting Beyond Your Capacity, Playing for Keeps, Lead Small, Creating a Lead Small Culture*, and his latest, *A New Kind of Leader* and *Don't Miss It.*

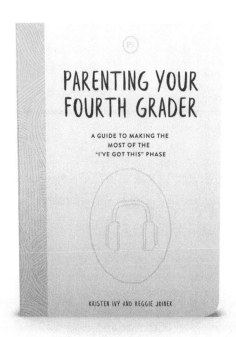

MAKE THE MOST OF EVERY PHASE IN YOUR CHILD'S LIFE

The guide in your hand is one of an eighteen-part series.

So, unless you've figured out a way to freeze time and keep your third grader from turning into a fourth grader, you might want to check out the next guide in this set.

Designed in partnership with Parent Cue, each guide will help you rediscover . . .

what's changing about your kid,
the 6 things your kid needs most,
and 4 conversations to have each year.

WANT TO GIFT A FRIEND WITH ALL 18 GUIDES
OR HAVE ALL THE GUIDES ON HAND FOR YOURSELF?

ORDER THE ENTIRE SERIES
OF PHASE GUIDES TODAY.